WOUNDS TO
WISDOM

WOUNDS TO WISDOM

Voices of Hope, Healing and
Redemption in the Face of Life's Challenges

TYE GRAYS

WOUNDS TO WISDOM
Copyright © 2024 Tye Grays
All rights reserved.

Published by Publish Your Gift®
An imprint of Purposely Created Publishing Group, LLC

No part of this book may be reproduced, distributed or transmitted in any form by any means, graphic, electronic, or mechanical, including photocopy, recording, taping, or by any information storage or retrieval system, without permission in writing from the publisher, except in the case of reprints in the context of reviews, quotes, or references.

Scriptures marked NIV are taken from the New International Version®. Copyright © 1973, 1978, 1984, 2011 by Biblica, Inc.™.
All rights reserved.

Scriptures marked KJV are taken from the Holy Bible, King James Version. All rights reserved.

Scriptures marked ESV are taken from English Standard Version®. Copyright © 2001 by Crossway, a publishing ministry of Good News Publishers. All rights reserved.

Scriptures marked NIVUK are taken from New International Version® Anglicized, NIV®. Copyright © 1979, 1984, 2011 by Biblica, Inc.®.
All rights reserved.

Printed in the United States of America

ISBN: 978-1-64484-640-7 (print)
ISBN: 978-1-64484-641-4 (ebook)

Special discounts are available on bulk quantity purchases by book clubs, associations and special interest groups. For details email: sales@publishyourgift.com or call (888) 949-6228.
For information logon to: www.PublishYourGift.com

This book is a collection of real-life stories.

The authors will share how they advanced their lives by overcoming personal impossible situations.

This book is dedicated to those who "crave" transformation.

I had to battle and conquer incredible odds.

TABLE OF CONTENTS

Foreword 1

From Darkness to Light:
A Journey of Faith and Freedom
Renee Moncito 3

God Appoints and Disappoints
Chaunté Humes 15

He Was Born a Miracle
Tye Grays 27

Teenage Mother
Catherine Head Kirkley 37

His Journey. My Journey. Our Journey.
Nikki Hardwick 55

Life as the First Generation Here
Frank Melendez 67

References 81

About the Authors 83

FOREWORD

"Trauma is an inescapable part of life. Regardless of your efforts to effectively deal with the challenges you face, sometimes all that can be done is to find meaning in the journey, as you painfully endure it," said Dr. Bessel Van Der Kolk, author of *The Body Keeps the Score*.[1] *Wounds to Wisdom* reads as a binding agent in a social setting, forging supportive connections between survivors. I would like to refer to the contributors in this book as "personal growth transformers." They share how trauma includes a realization of one's capabilities and resilience and a greater sense of the purpose for life. They take us through their journey from start to finish, emphasizing the various emotions felt and behaviors exposed as they became better equipped to work through their trauma.

These stories help us to realize that we are not alone; in fact, these traumatic events assist those who are encountering the same or similar experiences. Readers, use this book as a therapeutic survival toolkit to acknowledge the pain, suffering, and discomfort, and then come out "whole" on the other side with greater mental toughness, increased awareness, new perspectives, a better appreciation for life, and strengthened priorities.

We all love a comeback story, so why not share the ways in which you've faced great adversity and how you have bounced back!

God Bless!

Vicki Rice Jackson
Executive Director,
Coalition for Educational Partnerships

FROM DARKNESS TO LIGHT: A JOURNEY OF FAITH AND FREEDOM

By Renee Moncito

"Who hath delivered us from the power of darkness and hath translated us into the kingdom of his dear Son."

Colossians 1:13 (KJV)

Growing up in Haiti, a country with a history as vibrant as it is tumultuous, my family defied the odds. Despite being born into poverty, my parents instilled in me a sense of pride and self-esteem that radiated through our family. They were staunch advocates for the dignity and worth of all Black people, a legacy deeply rooted in Haiti's own history.

Haiti, the world's first Black-led republic to gain independence from European rule, had a complex past. From the revolutionary spirit of Toussaint L'Ouverture to the oppressive regime of François Duvalier, our nation's journey was marked by both valor and despair. While Duvalier, known as Papa Doc, used fear and mysticism to control the people, he also unwittingly fostered resilience and strength that flowed through our veins.

My father, a man of courage, commanded a group tasked with uncovering plots against Papa Doc. This group, known as the Tonton Macoute, was infamous for its brutal methods. Haiti lived under the shadow of fear, but my father saw a glimmer of light in the darkness. One fateful encounter with two stranded American missionaries would alter the course of his life.

On that ominous day, my father and his fellow Tonton Macoute members came across two White women and a stranded driver in the woods. Suspicion and unease hung heavy in the air. Why were these women there? Were they a threat to Papa Doc? The men debated their grim options, but my father volunteered to take responsibility.

Despite his limited English and the driver's inability to explain their presence, my father attempted to help. As night fell and the truck remained lifeless, the men's fear grew. My father faced an unthinkable decision—to carry out Papa Doc's orders and leave no witnesses or to defy his role.

It was then, in the darkest hour, that the unexpected happened. The two women began to pray, their voices pleading for mercy. They stretched their hands towards the broken-down truck, declaring their determination to live and fulfill the work of the Lord. My father, at a crossroads, made a choice—a choice that would lead to an unexpected miracle.

As the women prayed, the impossible unfolded before their eyes. The truck roared to life, defying all reason. It was a moment of transformation, a Damascus road experience that changed my father forever. He emerged from the shadows as a new man, one filled with hope, compassion, and a fervent faith in God.

My father's newfound purpose led him to share light in a land shrouded in darkness. Known as MaxeMo, he became an instrument of God, freeing the oppressed, breaking curses, and casting out demons. With my mother by his side, he embarked on missions to spread the message of Jesus, bringing healing and transformation to villages.

Yet, their journey was not without trials. An electrifying incident at a revival left my mother lifeless, a thunderstorm raging outside. Stranded in the mountains, the revival became a test of faith. But through unwavering prayer and an unexplainable return to life, her miraculous recovery spread like wildfire, unsettling the witch doctors, who thrived on fear.

As the witch doctors grew increasingly threatened, my family became a target. The missionaries devised a daring plan to get us out of Haiti, for our lives were in danger. Political turmoil, Papa Doc's regime, and the enmity of the witch doctors made our departure a matter of survival.

In the dead of night, we embarked on a perilous journey to America. I was just two years old, aware that something was amiss but oblivious to the gravity of our circumstances. The uncertainty, the fear, and the glimmer of hope surrounded us as we left our homeland behind.

We crossed oceans, mountains, and borders, traveling by plane, train, and bus. In a land foreign to us, we were welcomed with curiosity and kindness. I, a little girl speaking in French, became a source of fascination among the strangers who crossed our paths.

In this foreign land, we began anew, leaving behind a legacy of darkness and embracing a future filled with promise and faith. Our journey had taken us from darkness to light, from fear to hope, and it was just the beginning of an incredible adventure.

My journey unfolded within a house that stood as a beacon of hope and transformation for countless families. It was a place where new beginnings took root in a land of opportunity, where individuals could carve their destinies with unwavering self-determination bolstered by unwavering support. Our house was a sanctuary that kindled dreams and ignited the flames of aspiration, a place where hope thrived, nurturing futures filled with promise.

Within the walls of our house, a profound intersection of economic development and spiritual growth unfolded. This remarkable endeavor came at a cost, one borne by my dedicated parents. Their mission centered on the liberation of families and individuals left behind. Their tireless efforts spanned their work in local businesses, my mother's job, and their ministries that extended from church to church on weeknights and weekends. Amidst the constant influx of people seeking refuge in our home, I remained invisible.

I chose to silence my voice, gripped by fear that prevented me from divulging the painful truth of what transpired within our own home. It wasn't the potential judgment of my parents that deterred me, but the profound consequences I feared would follow. I dreaded the prospect of leaving the country, bidding farewell to the only life I had ever known, and losing the father I cherished.

My parents were oblivious to the torment I had endured at the hands of those who posed as allies within our own walls. To maintain the façade that all was well, I concealed the repeated violations I suffered. I knew that if my father discovered the truth, he would be consumed by anger. He would either destroy the house that stood as a symbol of our dreams or stand unwaveringly by my side, guiding me through the tumultuous process of reclaiming my stolen innocence.

The path I tread, characterized by my inability to trust my father, made me emotionally and spiritually relinquish him from the roles as priest, provider, and protector that he played in my life and compelled me to become those things for myself. I assumed the roles he could have fulfilled, becoming my own source of trust and protection, and simultaneously placed my trust in God.

My relationship with God remained a source of solace, a bond that nurtured my spirit, and an unshakable connection. He was my confidant, my sustenance, my very essence, and the focal point of my life. In His service, I ministered to His people in church, school, and the broader community. Yet, the closer I drew to Jesus in spirit, the more boldly I was attacked in the physical realm. I felt powerless, stripped of control, devoid of protection, and robbed of peace. The spiritual strength I possessed seemed to intensify my vulnerability in the physical world.

Faced with these trials, I embarked on a journey of transformation, seeking a way to shield my body while allowing my spirit to soar unencumbered. I grappled with the dreadful task of metamorphosis, navigating the challenging path of self-preservation and safety, all while endeavoring to safeguard the sanctuary of my soul. How would I accomplish this seemingly insurmountable feat?

Ever since then, I have been asked, "What's the plan?" "What's your insight?" "How did you gain this knowledge?" "How should we proceed?" These are the questions that still come my way daily. I've harnessed my superpowers, not just for self-preservation, but to build a fortress of financial strength and influence around me. I've proven that I'll take whatever measures necessary to shield myself from harm. I've released the grip of fear, for once you confront death without trepidation, it loses its dominion. I've learned to run toward fear, not away from it.

In crafting this life of mine, I've acquired not just material possessions and wealth but a set of invaluable skills that I can now articulate as strategy, negotiation, and leadership. I honed these abilities on the streets while managing a multi-million-dollar enterprise. In business, I have witnessed firsthand the depths to which individuals will sink for the allure of money. These observations led me to question authority, as I saw doctors, lawyers, judges, politicians, police officers, and executives commit unspeakable acts. It became clear that success wasn't about education, titles, or degrees; it was about character and integrity.

I discovered that every facet of life, regardless of how unusual or unconventional it may seem, is indeed a lifestyle. This alternative path grants access to the same opportunities as those who follow the conventional norms. The difference lies in the freedom to be authentic, unburdened by the need to impress or conform to societal expectations. I realized that most people have their own needs and are more than willing to extend a helping hand, guiding you from the shadows into the light to get that "bag."

This mindset transformed my acts of giving into something transactional, guided by agendas and predetermined outcomes. I gave to assert control, to secure my place at the table. As a woman, I also gave out of respect and honor. When your life revolves around transactions, each moment becomes a cherished experience because once the deal concludes, you swiftly move on to the next. You learn to keep a tight-knit crew where betrayal and disloyalty are met with the ultimate consequence—a passage to the afterlife.

However, all of this left me feeling empty. Regardless of whether I traveled in a limousine or enjoyed VIP privileges, there was always a lingering hangover. Money couldn't fill the void. Everything changed when I became a parent. That pivotal moment demanded explanations for the cars, the jewelry, and the extravagant clothing. I yearned to set an example, just as my parents had for me, and prevent my children from repeating my mistakes. The question that loomed was how I could leave it all behind and start anew, especially with the responsibilities of parenthood weighing on my shoulders.

I craved a fresh start, dreaming of enough money to go legit. The plan seemed foolproof: drop the kids, switch the cars, and regroup later. But doubts nagged at me. Did I leave the car in the right spot? Were the lights working? Boss lady's reassurances clashed with my unease.

The day arrived, and after dropping the kids, I initiated the car switch. What was meant to be routine turned into a robbery. The money wasn't there. Panic set in as we tracked them. Faced with a choice, I hesitated. Negotiations failed. Guilt consumed me. On my knees, I prayed for deliverance, for my kids' safety. The weekend brought stress and tears, and in my lowest moment, I heard God's whisper: "Let it go. I'll take care of you."

Friday and Saturday were the two longest days of my life. I was shedding the past and yearning for a better life for myself and my children. Then, Sunday arrived. I hadn't slept all night, my face puffy from crying, but I had to go to church. It was the day I surrendered my life to God. I felt like I was on cloud nine. Like a weight had been lifted.

What I realized is that after I surrendered my life, it didn't surrender my bills. I didn't know what to do. I just couldn't keep spending money without a game plan. Where would I go from here? Jeremiah 1:10 and Ecclesiastes 3:2 became the guiding lights on my journey. I had to go down, down to rise up, up. This transformation required renewing my mind, as Romans 12:2 (NIV) says, "Do not conform to the patterns of this world but be transformed by the renewing of your mind. Then you will be able to test and approve what God's will is—his pleasing and perfect will." It became clear that everything I loved about my life was hard work to maintain on my terms. When you let God work, it's enduring and sustainable, bringing the peace of God along with it.

I needed a revelation about my life's purpose. Jeremiah 1:10 (NIV) spoke to me: "See, today I appoint you over nations and kingdoms to uproot and tear down, to destroy and overthrow, to build and to plant." I knew I didn't want any more young girls, young adults, or women to experience what I had gone through. I just didn't know where to start or how. Yet, when God gives you a vision, He provides the means.

I found myself cruising in my Benz, immersed in the soulful sounds of the Gospel, courtesy of Fred Hammond's "Blessed." Meanwhile, an older, distinguished stranger piloting a sleek BMW was in a parallel musical universe with smooth jazz enveloping his car. Both of us were lost in our separate worlds, our respective tunes blasting.

Amidst the musical symphony, the distinguished gentleman noticed me, offering a friendly honk and a warm smile. As we continued down the road, his playful flirtations began to dance through the air, creating an unexpected connection in the rhythm of the moment. Undeterred, I pressed on, and to my surprise, he chose to follow me to a nearby restaurant, his eagerness evident as he extended an invitation to share lunch together.

During that lunch, he expressed his desire to buy a yacht. Being me, I tested him, and he revealed that he was serious. I offered to help him finance the boat, and in doing so, I uncovered his profession. He was a doctor of psychology with a master's in sociology. An older, sophisticated, and handsome man with a beautiful spirit. The old me would have dismissed him, but this new me saw him as a destiny partner. His candid sharing of his past, transforming from a dope fiend to an educated man, moved me to tears. It was like God had placed an example in front of me of someone I could become.

I brokered the yacht deal, gaining access to a beautiful yacht through him. We both benefited. I helped him with his credit, and he gave me guidance on starting a social service agency. It was a win-win. But this wasn't just about making money; it was about helping people and making a difference and impact in the lives of families.

As I prepared for the inspection of my new office space, God worked miracles. I secured four months of rent-free space, and people I didn't even know contributed furniture and computers on their credit cards. My friend even painted the night before. As I stood in my 800-square-foot office with three rooms, cozy and classy, I be the same.

My mission now was to dismantle the system and to confront rules and regulations that made no sense for families of color. I was no longer a bystander but a disrupter and change agent, tearing down and rebuilding, just as Jeremiah 1:10 foretold so that Proverb 14:26 could be realized: "In the fear of the LORD, there is strong confidence, and his children will have a place of refuge" (ESV).

I know that walking this path of the journey to which I've been called is impossible without the guidance and support of the Holy Spirit. It's a realization that comes from deeply understanding passages like Isaiah 55:8-9, which reminds us that God's ways are not our ways, and Ephesians 3:20-21, which speaks of God's ability to do far more than we can imagine. Every experience, every tear, every pain, is not in vain. As Jeremiah 29:11 assures us, God has plans for our prosperity and hope.

Recognizing and believing in your unique gift and talent is crucial, as Proverbs 18:16 tells us that our gifts can make room for us in this world. We don't need to chase after money or influential people; we just need to nurture and use our God-given talents, and the divine attraction will align the right opportunities and people with us (1 Peter 4:10).

Staying rooted in God's word and allowing the Holy Spirit to work within us helps us focus on our divine calling amidst the noise of the world. Proverbs 2:3-5 encourages us to seek discernment and knowledge. It's essential to realize that as you develop your journey, you'll encounter various people who may serve different roles in your life. There are confidants, those rare individuals you can fully trust, constituents who align with your cause, and comrades who support your mission in the fight. Understanding their motives is key to maintaining healthy relationships and fortifying your heart so you won't become bitter. Proverbs 4:23 says, "Above all else, guard your heart for everything you do flows from it" (NIVUK).

When you finish one assignment and move on to the next, remember Philippians 4:13: "I can do all things through Christ who strengthens me" and Daniel 11:32: "But the people that do know their God shall be strong and do exploits" (KJV). Embrace your season, for it's your time to go forth with the mission you've been commanded to fulfill. For now, you have been translated from darkness to light and will embark on your journey of faith and freedom.

GOD APPOINTS AND DISAPPOINTS

By Chaunté Humes

When I was a little girl, my parents instilled in me that doing well in school was very important if I wanted to have a "happy" and "prosperous" future. They, along with my entire family, left Central America to escape violence, poverty, and scarce opportunities in search for a chance at a better life. Like so many immigrants to the United States, they subscribe to the belief that education is the golden ticket for the oppressed and downtrodden. They aren't entirely wrong, but they aren't entirely right either.

Allow me to explain myself. For a long time, my identity was wrapped up in being a high achiever and in how far I could excel academically rather than in nurturing the talents and passions that come naturally to me. Let me tell you, the excel rut has been exhausting. Being told for so long to excel with no real compass to help me navigate where I was going has led to complete and utter burnout. I'm tired. Yet somehow, someway, I persevere. I persevere in the face of missteps, spirit breakers (naysayers), and soul-crushing tragedies.

Now my parents aren't the sole architects of the identity I've clung to my entire life. However, they helped to construct the foundation of my identity and how I suspect most other people view me: intelligent, capable, resilient, responsible, and a doer. Over time, the foundation of my identity has been built up by a community of people—educators, life-long friends, family, and siblings—who have molded my sense of self and my core values, including family, faith, human kindness, hard work, generosity, security, and happiness, just to name a few.

When I was about nine or ten years old, I once overheard my fourth-grade teacher analogize my performance in class to my parents. He said to them, "She washes the dishes, but she doesn't sweep the floors and wipe down the counters." He offered no real support or guidance on what could be done to help improve my alleged "average" performance. At that age, most kids would have not understood, would have dismissed, or entirely ignored the comment. But I had a keen sense of discerning unfavorable remarks from adults. It isn't lost on me that it was God who was guiding my feelings and bestowing upon me the ability to trust in my intuition at a very young age. Although my young brain couldn't fully articulate what I was feeling, I now realize it was hurt and shame. My teacher's confidence in my abilities didn't match the confidence my parents had in me, and their confidence in me was gold. In my mind, his assessment of my work was an assessment of me, and it was negative and untrue. And sure, he may have meant well, but words are powerful.

Words can either uplift or discourage a young mind. So, I chose to refute his words. From then onward, I set out to achieve and to prove my intelligence, but most importantly, to soar high above the spirit breakers. I vividly recall this memory because it's where I learned to be resilient. This memory for me was a critical point in my story where I embraced my future identity and my parents' hopes for me. It's where I began to assume the appointed role of "smart daughter with a bright future." I don't know if that's sad or applaudable, but it is all a part of what has poured into the foundation of who I am. Thankfully, the experience has lived up to its purpose in my life, thus far.

Not all my educational experiences have been like that of my fourth-grade experience. Fortunately, I have been a student (mentee) of a host of top-tier, genuinely supportive, and diverse educators, many of whom I still maintain strong relationships with. I'm in deep gratitude to each of them for their unwavering commitment to being exemplary stewards of education in an inner-city public-school system that often lacks the needed resources to enrich and improve the lives of all its students.

My biggest and longest supporters have truly been my family—I have a *huge* family—and my friends whom I consider to be my bonus extended family. I'm blessed to have strong bonds with some of the most down-to-earth, intelligent, kind, caring, and creative group of women. Our friendships span over two decades and counting. We've cheered each other on through some of life's greatest milestones, we've cried together during some of life's hardest trials, and we steadfastly show up for one another. By the grace of God, I've had the distinct pleasure of observing my friends transform from young women to strong, self-reliant, and ambitious grown women. I'm truly thankful for our sisterhood. Like my God-given family, my friends continuously show me how to keep moving forward when life gets uncertain and hard.

At this point, you may be wondering, "What in the world does any of this have to do with God appointing and disappointing?" Well, this is the part of my story where all the love and support of my community and all my lived experiences (of mistakes, missteps, rising above, and persevering) along the way converge to help me get through one of the most heartbreaking experiences of my life.

I was appointed by God to be a daughter, granddaughter, little sister, niece, and eventually, someone's friend. I was born into the protection of my parents and my two older brothers. When I was eleven years old, God gave me a new and exciting promotion: big sister. I had always wanted a sister—someone with whom to go on adventures, someone with whom to do life, and someone with whom to grow old. Another girl would also even out our sibling proportion: two boys and two girls. Looking back, anticipating her arrival was really an exciting time. I don't recall my mom having a baby shower, but I do recall us picking out the cutest baby clothes and toys. I had the distinct honor of picking out her middle name. I must admit, I was worried about our large age gap, but when she arrived, it felt like a dream fulfilled.

God gave me someone I had always wanted. She was cute, independent, and brainy. She was a joy to be around and had a smile that could truly light up any room. Everyone adored her. Our mom made us take countless photos together when we were younger, especially during the holidays. There's a photo of us we took one Christmas. It's one of my favorites. She had to be about four years old. In the photo, she's standing next to me smiling from ear to ear in a velvet red and pink Christmas dress. Her hair is pulled half up and half down, she has three little Shirley Temple curls draping her forehead, and she has traditional Belizean gold leaf earrings in her ears. In this photo, like in most of our photos, happiness is beaming from her in every direction like sun rays, and she looks so proud.

In looking back on this moment, I believe her joy may have come from us being together. She wanted to go everywhere with me, and if she could, she would. Sometimes it would annoy me, but I'm so happy that she did. Along the way, we made so many great memories like celebrating her birthday at Disneyland, planning her high school prom party, and sending her off to college.

When you're young, you don't realize how fast time flies and how much you take for granted in that time. I wish I had done so much more with my sister. I wish I had been a lot more intentional about planning and spending time with her when she was away for college. I wish I had better understood that not everyone carries the same mental fortitude and toughness to get through life's obstacles and challenges. I wish I had been a lot kinder and understanding of my baby sister. I wish that the reality of her passing, of her deciding to take her own life, never was.

On Sunday, March 5, 2023, my entire world changed. It started out as an ordinary Sunday. I got up, showered, dressed, and made plans with my partner to go shopping for groceries in preparation for the week ahead. On my way out, I briefly spoke with my father in the kitchen. He let me know that my sister wasn't feeling well in Georgia and that she had been to the emergency room in the early morning. She was home resting now, and eventually our cousin would stop by the house to drop her some medicine prescribed by the ER doctor.

I didn't think much of it when my father shared this with me. My sister had been going through a rollercoaster of illness over the past two years. She suddenly had these long bouts of crippling stomach issues that caused her to be unable to keep down food and water. She must've been to the emergency room nearly a hundred times in that period, and she went on countless doctor's visits with no cure in sight.

Doctors eventually diagnosed her with gastroparesis, a kind of neurological stomach paralysis in which your food doesn't digest fast enough. To be honest, it didn't make any sense. How does one contract such an illness? None of the doctors could give us a clear explanation. When my sister would become ill, she became noticeably ill. She would be in crippling pain, unable to coherently talk or barely even walk. It was so hard watching her endure this illness. Her weight constantly fluctuated during this period. She was cautioned by doctors to stay away from greasy foods, alcohol, and marijuana use, which would trigger her condition. She did her very best to follow the doctor's orders.

In the months leading up to her death, she had been doing so well. She had a routine down, she was excelling at work, and her illness seemed to subside a bit. As a family, we were all excited for her. It seemed like that hard period in our lives, in her life, especially, was now under control. She was even well enough to travel during this period. She secured her passport and took a trip to our native home of Belize with my father and cousins. She seemed to love every minute of exploring the place where our entire family came from. I was truly sad I couldn't make the trip with her, but in my head, I began to plan future adventures for the two of us. We had never traveled together, and because I know firsthand just how energizing experiencing a new place can be for a novice traveler, I wanted to do that with my baby sister. In my heart, I was so excited about the idea.

It seemed at the time that we could all worry just a little bit less about my baby sister. In hindsight, it's hard to not feel like I (as her big sister) should have known better. Though she and I never talked about her feelings on the experience she had endured over the past two years, I suspect now that being sick for so long had taken a toll on her mentally and physically. The effects of being in lockdown during COVID during this period and the isolation it brought to all our lives certainly may have had a deeper impact on my sister and her outlook on the future.

While in the grocery store, I received numerous missed calls from my mom. It didn't appear unusual at first. If my parents don't get me on the first call, they usually call a second, and a third time. When I finally picked up, my mom asked through tears if I could come back to the house. I still didn't think anything of it. I told her I would be on my way, and we hung up. It wasn't until she called me again and I picked up that I realized something had to be truly wrong. She said my sister's name. It then became apparent to me as I was in the checkout line that I needed to get home to my parents. I high-tailed it out of the grocery store and had my partner drive me straight home.

In these days and times, we have the fortunate (or unfortunate) ability through our camera doorbells to keep a close watch on our homes. My first instinct was to check our camera doorbell in Georgia to see if I could get a visual on what was going on. What I saw outside our home, all the way from California, will stay with me my entire life. It was a scene of complete chaos. I saw red flashing lights everywhere, paramedic trucks, police cars, and personnel walking in and out of our home. I caught a glimpse of my cousin on the front porch crying her eyes out. I knew then that something terrible had transpired. I watched the scene outside our Georgia home on our camera doorbell phone all the way up until I reached the house. The pain I saw in my parents' eyes when I arrived said it all. My heart sank as they explained to me what had happened. Although I understood, I just couldn't believe it.

Detectives and family were calling my parents now. I knew I needed to help my parents, but as our family quickly filled our living room, my brain became unplugged. I had to rely on my neighbors to book us a flight to Georgia because for some reason, in that moment, a task so simple became incredibly hard to do. My brain froze from the shock of the news, but I eventually broke through. I knew we needed to get to my sister, to Georgia, as quickly as possible.

Fortunately, we secured a straight flight that landed at 6 a.m. the next morning. I didn't sleep the whole five-hour plane ride. I worried about my parents and desperately wanted to be near my sister. I booked a car and hotel for us so that we didn't have to worry about transportation from the airport or lodging even though I knew that no matter the situation, there was no way my parents would stay in a hotel if we had a home to go to. So, we landed in Georgia and went straight to our home. My father and I got out of the car and went into the house first. The tire marks from the dirt from the gurney used to carry my sister out of our home to the coroner's office was a sobering reminder of our new reality.

The week we spent in Georgia talking to detectives and the coroner seemed like forever. As the days marched on, I became more and more anxious to see my sister. I worried about my parents and did my best to protect and support them. No parent should have to be faced with burying their child. So, I carried this heavy load for them. I made the calls and took care of all the planning for the funeral service.

Every intricate detail for my sister's sendoff, I handled with the help of my family and friends. Putting together her obituary proved to be immensely emotional—even more emotional than preparing her hair and makeup for her sendoff. I had planned or helped to plan so many other things for my sister. Never did I ever imagine that I'd be planning her funeral, especially not in my thirty-fifth year and her twenty-fourth year of life. I took precise care to make it beautiful for her. I'm thankful to God for everyone who showed kindness, support, and generosity during this time. Through each and every one of those individuals, God seemed to be showing up and showing out for our family during one of our darkest hours.

Just about everyone who knew my little sister attended the funeral. Family, neighbors, my friends, my older siblings' friends, my parents' friends, and educators were all in attendance to say their goodbyes. The chapel was filled from wall to wall, and every seat was filled. Many wore pink to honor my sister. It's bittersweet to see how much funerals bring people together.

I hadn't realized how full the room was until I stood up to speak at the podium. Even though my heart was hurting, I felt comforted by everyone in attendance. It made me think of how much I wished my sister knew she was loved by everyone there that day. As I sat listening to family and friends take turns sharing memories of my sister at the podium, I was quickly set in even more awe of my sister. The night before, I had spent some hours writing a small eulogy for my sister, and on the day of her funeral, everyone at the podium seemed to echo my exact thoughts about her. Our special memories of her all revealed the same thing—she was truly special. Though it brought tears to my eyes, it made my heart smile and feel a little lighter.

My uncle graciously accepted the responsibility of leading the services and formally eulogizing my sister. In his sermon, he reminded everyone in the chapel that we are all here "on purpose," meaning no matter our differences, trials, and tribulations, God or the universe has conspired for us to be here. Although we don't always feel as though we've realized our purpose in this life, the truth is that our "being" here is purposeful. We all have been appointed a purpose, and it could be as simple as being a son or a daughter, a parent, a spouse, a sibling, or a friend. Honor those appointments because they are invaluable. People are invaluable. I now understand what it truly means to be disappointed. You can't be disappointed unless you've been appointed to something. I was appointed as a big sister, and while I know I'll always be a big sister, that appointment has ceased.

In the aftermath of my sister's death, I've struggled with crippling anxiety and sadness trying to navigate this new identity and new reality. Grieving a loss from suicide is unique from any other loss. It's a rollercoaster of emotions that bubble up at inopportune times. A thick fog of anger and deep sorrow are staples of this grief. I've leaned heavily on my resilience to guide me through the last six months. Seeking help from my therapist and being open with friends about my day-to-day struggles has helped. Forcing myself to do the things I don't want to do, like getting out of bed somedays, has been part of the remedy.

Seeking out other resources and support groups has made the difference for me. Believe it or not, there are thousands of podcasts that deal with and discuss grief and where survivors discuss what they have done to get through it. I've also found that seeking out connection with other survivors of suicide loss has been deeply helpful because being a *survivor* can feel lonely. As a survivor, you're cautious about who you share your story with because you know not everyone will be genuinely empathetic. For this reason, the act of giving and receiving support from people who can relate to your exact feelings and emotions provides immense encouragement to find healthy ways to live with the loss.

If you're reading this and know someone struggling with depression or suicidal ideation, or you've lost someone to suicide, please know that there are hope, help, and resources available for you or anyone in need. The American Foundation for Suicide Prevention (https://afsp.org) is a non-profit organization dedicated to suicide prevention and support. They are committed to helping everyone find the resources they need to get better. If you are or anyone you know is in crisis, I urge you to please call the national suicide crisis line at 988 at any time of the day.

I pray for healing in all our lives.

HE WAS BORN A MIRACLE

By Tye Grays

My son was ejected from me on August 17, 1992. His due date was originally October 31, 1992. It will always be a day I can never forget. It was traumatizing. It was a bright summer day. The scents of honeysuckle glazed the air. It was hot, and my belly was fat. I would often say, "I wish to have him early." Little did I know what I was about to witness. Only God could show me the way out of this trauma. I made a decision to rely on my faith in God and trust that He could pull me through such adversity.

I was alone and afraid. As a new mommy, I had to get up and be strong, even though doctors hesitated so many times when I asked if he was even going to make it. I now regret it, but here's what happened.

It was a Monday, my day off from working in the salon. It was a normal day full of errands. I lived close to 31 Flavors, our neighborhood ice cream shop. I made a habit of going to get my favorite strawberry ice cream. My baby kicked every time we ate it. I got as much as I possibly could, so I got a cone with two scoops and darted off in the flow of LA traffic. I made my last run to the post office. By this time, it was mid-afternoon, LA traffic was congested per usual, and I had some bomb side streets I would often use to get around the city fast. I normally take my time on my day off, but on this particular day, I had to move swiftly. I had plans for the evening, so my time was limited.

At about 5:30 p.m., all that running around had me exhausted. I was overdue for a nap. I couldn't wait to get those clothes off. I often wore oversized fits. I used outfits from my wardrobe and made them fit comfily. To me, it was such a waste to spend money on maternity clothes. I knew I'd never wear them again. I didn't like anything tight on me. I felt like I was being smothered. I wasn't too belly flashy. I covered up. I had button down shirts from Guess, Damage, and Polo and anything cute and flowy. My pot belly was huge for six and a half months. Comfy was a must.

I took my clothes off, lay down, and woke up. About an hour went by, and I woke up feeling great and refreshed. It was something about those quick cat naps during pregnancy that made you feel so good. Time was slipping away. It was getting close to the time I was going to leave. I jumped up, grabbed my phone to confirm the night was still on, and I ran hot water lavender soaks and hopped in the bathtub. I enjoyed bath time during pregnancy. It was alone time and bonding time with my baby. We were both always soothed in there. I could get stuck in it for hours sometimes, but not this night. I had big plans to hang out, so it was time to get out.

On my way, I went to pick up my friends to go hangout. Before going, I had to make a stop to get some gas. On arrival at the gas station, there was a very uncomfortable feeling that came over me. In a split second, I was caught in gun fire. I was in a full-blown shootout. The blow to the stomach was all I remembered. My mind and my heart were moving so fast in this moment. I was in shock from the excruciating pain of being struck. My mind was working overtime to reconcile the reality of what had just happened to me and my baby.

Without hesitation, I began to calm myself and breathe slowly. I had been breathing fast, and my heart had been beating like a drum and pounding over and over, but there was no time to play in this critical situation. So, I had a chance to remember to breathe for myself and my unborn child. All I knew was if I panicked, I would lose him. Blood was leaking from everywhere, and the hot bullets that pierced my skin left me numb to nothing but hot, blazing fire to feel.

Seconds felt like minutes. Time was moving so slowly. All I could think was, "Is my baby is going to die?" I just kept repeating to myself over and over, "This can't be happening right now."

God immediately came to me and spoke to me, and I heard His words very clearly. He told me to fight. He told me to fight for my life so I could be forever blessed. He told me to fight and breathe. "Breathe slowly, and don't be afraid. You have no time to lose. I'm here, and I will be with you all the way," He said. I had an out-of-body experience. I watched myself in that moment and decided that I would fight with each breath to keep us alive. I just continued to focus on my breathing. And that's what I did. I maintained my breathing until I got in the ambulance. When I saw the paramedics, a sense of calm came over me. I felt safe. I knew I'd be okay for some reason. So, I took a very deep breath and put trust in these guys because that's all I had at that point.

The ride was a crazy experience to say the least. The paramedics were nice, but they were moving fast and trying to pretend that I was okay. They were treating me with the oxygen mask, giving me IVs, and bandaging me with gauze. They were on the phone with dispatchers deciding on which hospital to take me to. Everything started to move slowly to me. I was in and out. I just made sure I focused on my breathing, never mind the pain. I wanted my baby to be calm. I had control of that, so I kept up my breathing. That was my true focus in the ambulance.

When I arrived at the ER unit, I had a white sheet pulled over me. My shirt was cut off by the guy in the ambulance. So, my belly was quite exposed, and all I heard was people screaming and shouting in disbelief when they saw my pregnant belly and the gunshots to it. The gurney was moving fast through the hospital. All I could see were people's faces just staring down at me and the bright hospital lights. It made me more alert and kept me focused. So, we got in the elevators to take me to emergency surgery. All I can remember was the emergency staff taking off my jewelry.

Everything was moving so fast. They put so many monitors and IVs in me. They were checking on the baby's status the whole time while attending to me. I was in chaos for sure. I remember the last order given to me, which was "Count backwards from ten to zero."

I woke up to a bright and busy facility. Blankets were so tight around me and very warm. I remember a nurse waking me up to ask me how I was feeling. I told her, "I guess I'm alright. But did that really happen to me?"

She replied, "Yes, ma'am, that really happened to you!"

And this was when it got real for me. I had no choice but to totally use my faith in God to continue to get me through.

What got me through was Peter 5:11 (KJV): "But the God of All Grace, who hath called us unto his eternal glory by Christ Jesus, after that ye has suffered for a while, make you perfect stablish, strengthen, settle you. To him be glory and dominion forever and ever. Amen."

I was up in intensive care, and a busy nursing staff was working around the unit. I couldn't talk. Tubes were in my mouth. I had so many questions. Yet, I was silent with nothing to say. Eventually, I was approved by a sweet nurse who was ready to administer me medication in my IV. I didn't like medication, so I asked her all about it. She let me know it was for my healing process, so I agreed. I had so many more things to ask. However, I saved them for later.

I was told it was almost time to remove the tubes in my mouth. They went down to my stomach during surgery. It was so uncomfortable just sitting in my body. I suffered so much pain during this time. I often called on God when I was alone. My prayers would last for hours sometimes. I mostly prayed about going downstairs to neonatal intensive care to see my baby boy.

They finally took me downstairs to remove the tube in my mouth. Once it was removed, I was ready for recovery. Next was to go meet my son. I couldn't do that until I was able to get better, which included me talking, walking, breathing, and enduring these horrible bullet wounds that left me in excruciating pain. My son was in ICU with the babies on another floor, so I had no choice but to get strong on so many levels. Physically, I needed to find the courage and strength to get up out of the hospital bed and walk after undergoing extensive surgery. But mentally, I was struggling really hard. God kept showing up at my most difficult times. I would often ask God to please speed up my healing process so I could go meet my baby. All I could think of every day was "What if I don't see him? What if he dies? What if he slips away from me and I never see him?"

"What kind of shit is this?" I thought. I had to gather myself and let each day that went by be my motivation for the next few weeks. Each day, I got stronger and stronger. Eventually, I was walking slowly, but I was back on my feet. God gave me the strength again to walk slowly. I thanked my nursing staff every day. They were so attentive and nice to me in the hospital.

The next day, I got up and felt pretty good. I asked to go see my baby, so they checked with my doctor, and he okayed me to go see my child downstairs. They ordered me a wheelchair and prepared to take me down. I was so happy this day came. I could finally see whom I gave birth to. I had heard so much about him. My mom and dad, especially, would tell me how beautiful and strong he was. My mom told me he was so cute with so much hair. That's when I figured out why I had suffered so much heartburn during pregnancy, but that's another story for another time.

I was finally on my way to the elevators, and it was a very bumpy ride. My stomach was in a lot of pain from the surgery. I still had gauze and tubes from drainage still in me, so the experience to see him was not a comfortable one, but it was a choice I made, and it had to be done.

I made it to neonatal ICU and saw all the babies in incubators. Some looked okay, and some looked very sick. Some were huge, some were small. As I rode past all of them in the wheelchair, I couldn't help but be amazed at my very own situation. I snapped out of it, prayed for those little babies, and finally came upon mine. He was there in his incubator lying down on his side, looking at me being wheeled in by my mom. She said, "There he is." As she kept pushing me closer to him, I remember tears falling down my face, looking at him. My very first time seeing him, I understood what faith looked like. I saw what life and death looked like all at one time. In this situation, I learned to believe that God is real.

My son was so little. I asked the nurse if I could pick him up. She said, "Okay. Yes, Momma, you can hold him for a short while." I washed my hands up while she disconnected some of the monitors stuck to him. He was so wired up, I could barely hold him well. I did the best I could. I held him, and we stared into each other's eyes as to say, "Hey, there you are." My baby was so little and perfect. He looked like a little potato. He had a big head, though I knew some day he would grow into it.

A few weeks went by before we first saw each other again. He was everything and more than I could imagine. Though, as a young, twenty-one-year-old, first-time mommy, I was devastated by how my baby was delivered to me. For him to be a preemie with such a terrorizing traumatic entrance in the world, he sure was a miracle. And that's exactly what the nurses and doctors called my baby—miracle baby. He made it through the odds.

As I continued to recover in the hospital, I got word that my baby had to go through many complications and surgeries. He had a much longer stay in the hospital than I did. I was torn to shreds when I found out he wasn't going home with me. How can you carry your baby and leave the hospital without him? It just didn't feel fair. I needed the doctors to do more for me, for him, but the process didn't work that way.

My mom brought the Bible to the hospital all the time, and for some strange reason, I totally resented it. I told her to stop bringing it. I asked her "why" so many times. "Why do bring this Bible, Momma?"

She would always say, "So we can stay close to God." And that scared me. It made me feel like God was going to take my baby. It made me have anxiety attacks. But as time went by, I started to understand my mother's approach with the Bible. I later learned it was to soothe us all. To cover my baby and me with the spirit of God. To connect our bodies with the Word. And that it did.

God had favor over me, and in the early days on my journey to healing, I trusted in Him to get me through the process. I felt the pressure to survive for me and my baby. Most don't live through such tragic situations as my own, especially sharing it with an unborn child. I had to be strong for the both of us. I made it through with God, prayer, and so many loved ones, some of whom are here and some of whom are no longer here. They all kept me grounded and so grateful to see another day. I relied on each and every person who supported me and came to see them as a life jacket. They held me up even when they didn't know it. I was overwhelmed by the many blessings in the hospital. I had so much to be thankful for.

Now that I have overcome that trauma in my life, I realize it was just a journey that welcomed me in my today's life. I'm much stronger today than I ever was because of the experience. I am wise with my decisions, and my focus is enriched with knowledge.

Now today as an adult woman, I can say I take none of what I have gone through for granted. Life is a real blessing. One day at a time is a real thing. I live by it. In great moments in your life, you will always remember to trust the process one day at a time. It took time and effort to come out of the dark space I was in after the birth of my son. With postpartum, fear and anger traveled with me for the most part. I changed and gained strength later. I had to learn to trust again, and that was going to take one day at a time. I had a few setbacks, but they didn't stop me. I used my setbacks to get me to move forward. I no longer hold grudges against myself for dealing with trauma. I now walk forward and use my past as a steppingstone to keep moving forward. I pray we all get past our traumas and heal.

TEENAGE MOTHER

By Catherine Head Kirkley

It was June 1964, and I had just graduated from Joel Elias Springan High School. The summer was ahead, and my friends and I would party to our hearts' content. By September, most of my friends were working or in school. I was still without a plan for what was next. At my parents' insistence, I took the SAT so that I would be eligible for my next step, Howard University, but that was not to be. I was pregnant.

Stunned, shocked, and speechless, I didn't know what to do. Never in my life had I been so scared, so lost. Marriage was a no-go. How would I tell these people who had put their everything into me that I was pregnant? So many thoughts ran through my mind. Whom could I tell? Where could I go? What would they say? Fear immobilized me. Whom could I trust? To whom could I turn?

It would be months before my father confronted me. We were eating dinner, and he said, "You look pregnant." I was devastated. I was speechless. I had written my parents a letter, but I hadn't delivered it, and now I had come face to face with the truth. My father's disappointment was unmistakable in his tone and look. My mother was so gentle and loving.

God knew what I needed. Of course, I was not the first girl in my family to get pregnant outside of marriage, but I was his daughter, and this was not acceptable.

I had gone to an obstetrician with a girlfriend, and he told me that I was pregnant and it was too late to abort. I had never thought of an abortion because I had never come to terms with being pregnant, though all the signs were there. My mother knew because I told my cousin Eddie, and I'm sure, not knowing what to do, he confided in his mother, my mother's sister. Now that the whole family knew, the community knew, what would be my next step?

My mother, the trooper, the planner, would find a doctor in Virginia to become my obstetrician. My mother and aunt, meanwhile, were facing another crisis. My grandmother, Nana, was terminally ill. I didn't know it or realize it, probably because I was so caught up in my own life's circumstances. My Nana, hearing how harshly my father received the news, would once again come to my rescue.

Though seriously ill, Nana would get up off of her deathbed to call me. She wanted me to know that she loved me and that everything was going to be okay. I never got to see or hear her voice, but her words, her love, and her empathy for me resonates today. I cannot remember a time in my life when my road was tough that she did not come back to me to tell me she loved me and that it was going to be okay. My Nana passed on April 13, 1965, and my child was born six weeks later. Though she never got to see my baby, she gave me the strength to carry on.

No one was as magnificent as my mother. She walked every step with me. She never said anything that would suggest she wasn't proud of me. Everything I am today is because I had a "mother" in the true sense of the word.

In addition to having the best mother, I had a village. Long before Hillary Clinton spoke of a village, God gave me one. My aunt and her husband welcomed my baby with open arms. Everyone rallied around me. After all, I was on my way; I had been accepted to Howard.

My parents divorced when my baby was five months old. It wasn't a surprise to anyone who knew them. It was time for my mother, who had sacrificed all her life for others, to have some joy.

My aunt and my mother, as they had done years before when they were young women, made a pact. My mother would continue to work, and my aunt would keep my baby during the week while I went to school. This was the same aunt who kept me while my mother worked when I was a baby.

My girlfriends and guy friends would all step up to be godparents to my baby. My baby was an adorable one, and everyone signed up to help me out. One girl I had known since elementary school would be my baby's official godmother. She really loved this little girl, and from the day she was born, her absolute devotion to her would be omnipresent.

The guys with whom I hung would become her godfathers, and all would lend a hand in making sure the baby was surrounded by love and guidance. I was the first in my crew to be a parent. All eyes were on me, and all hands were on deck. I was ready to go.

When I walked onto Howard's campus in September 1965, my baby was four months old. Before she was one, she would be twirling on the quad. My every thought, every move, and every decision were centered on this sweet, precious, and beautiful little girl who called me "Mommie." I loved her so, and she would be the reason I would make it through.

Campus life would be different for me. I was a mother and student. I had responsibilities beyond my classes and college life. I would make the adjustments, and I would focus on my one goal: graduation. Classmates at Howard had come from around the world and country. Most were focused on college life. They lived in the dorms, ran for student council, played on the teams, and hung out together in their dorms and the student union. I was a city girl and a mother, and my time after class was spent taking care of my class load and my baby.

Not many people on campus knew I was a mother, and so as they became sorors and leaders of the class, I concentrated on my classes. Howard was known for attracting the best and brightest. Girls came to get both a degree and a Mrs. in front of their names. Those were not my goals. Mine was to graduate so I could take care of my baby.

I did get to know my classmates, and a few are my friends today. There were those guys and girls on campus who would stand out because they ran for homecoming or student council, or they played sports. Howard's homecoming is still the talk of DC. I only went to one, and that was the year before I was a student there. My Saturdays after class were spent with my baby.

My intro to Howard's campus was Freshman Assembly. It was 1:40 on a Tuesday at Cramton Auditorium. Every freshman had to attend. You had an ID number and an assigned seat. It was a Humanities Lecture. We were told to look to our right and left because someone was not going to be there to graduate. The university was serious about this orientation, as I witnessed seniors taking this class. It was then that I knew graduation was not promised, it was earned.

I was enrolled in the School of Liberal Arts. I had chosen sociology as my major, but there would be a curriculum of classes I would have to take before I would get to my major.

From my first year at Howard, I knew summer school would be a part of my life. Six weeks of my summer would be dedicated to classes that I needed to graduate. I was a full-time student with full-time responsibilities as a mother.

For six of my eight semesters at Howard, I would have Tuesday, Thursday, and Saturday classes. I would go out to my aunt's house and pick up my baby so that I could spend time with her on the weekends. My mother would keep my baby on Saturday mornings until my classes were over.

Like my parents had done with me, I spent the weekends with my child. I never went anywhere that she couldn't go. We were inseparable. My mother bought me a car on my nineteenth birthday so I could meet my obligations with ease. She thought of everything.

As a sociology major, my junior year at Howard found me at Junior Village doing my field work assignment. It was a facility that kept children whose parents were unable to care for them until they were able to document that they could provide for their children. These children, by law, were unadoptable.

Our assignment was to select two families and do a case study on them. We were to choose children from different backgrounds.

My Thursdays in the spring of 1968 were spent at Junior Village. That assignment was one of the most defining moments in my life. Oddly enough, I still remember both families. I still have my paperwork, and their names are carved in my memory bank. The children were sweet. I will not disclose their names, but I will always remember them. Let's refer to them as Family A and Family B.

Family A was a family of six, and the two younger children were placed together in a dorm-like atmosphere. The little girl was six, and she would tell me every week that her "Mommie" was coming for them. Her brother would always be standing in the entryway waiting for whoever was to come to greet them. As we took them on trips, he would sit on my lap and call me "Mommie." He didn't see race. I was Black, and he was White. All he saw was love.

Family B was from Maryland. The mother was White, and the two fathers were Black. The mother couldn't take them home because mixed-race children were unacceptable. Both children were subdued. Sadness permeated their being. Their eyes carried the sadness of abandonment. My heart bore the weight of a mother who could not imagine what it would be like not to keep my baby.

My junior year at Howard was a year like no other. In April 1968, Dr. Martin Luther King, Jr. was assassinated in Memphis, Tennessee. The streets of DC went wild. Places that had been safe havens were now a disaster zone. Streets that I navigated from school to home were now occupied territories. For the first time since the Civil War, troops inhabited our city. The National Guard had been called in. They set up stations throughout our city. I had evening classes, and the city was under martial law. You couldn't be on the streets after a certain hour; a curfew had been instituted. If you broke curfew, you would be detained. Those of us who were students carried our schedule and school ID just in case all hell broke out.

My child would turn three that year, and though we would celebrate, we knew things would never be the same. Before the semester was over that June, I heard the news from California on my way to class that Robert Kennedy had been assassinated. I could not believe it.

As I had been for two years, I would be in summer school. My goal was to graduate on time, and it would take three summer schools and eight semesters to assure that goal. Our lives had been colored by the times we lived in. Our generation, the baby boomers, had seen perhaps more violence in our streets and on television than any generation before. Almost in unison, we could recite the lives lost in our quest for a new day, a new America. It did not come cheaply, and lives lost ran across all racial, ethnic, religious, and economic lines.

Most of us remembered Emmett Till, the boy who whistled at a White woman and whose body was found in the Tallahatchie River. We remember the open casket his mother dared to show so all the world would know what they had done to her child. We remembered Mississippi because death was inevitable there. We saw Medgar Evers shot down in the driveway of his home. We heard stories and saw newsreels of the students who dared to go on Freedom Rides or sit-ins at lunch counters in the segregated South. These were our peers, our generation, who were picking up the tab. It both frightened and emboldened us. We needed a change, and whether it started on a bus or a college campus, our resolve was solidified by our determination to live a fuller life. The chants of our generation were reverberating across the world. We were the difference.

My junior year at Howard had been marked by the Class of '68. Our friends, our classmates, and our peers were determined to join the chorus for change. 1968 was a turning point. That class was determined to make things better, to create a world where the distance between those who lived near Howard and those who attended Howard would no longer be light years apart.

The Class of 1968 set the tone and passed the baton to our class, the Class of 1969. We cannot measure or adequately give credit to those in '68 who gave the last full measure of their commitment to change. We can, however, say we stayed the course.

It was our turn to step up, stand up, and speak up for what we knew was right and just. I didn't live on campus, and so the fire of those who did inspired me to do my part. More than anything, I wanted to graduate. I was reminded by those who were committed and knowledgeable that the stakes were higher than my own personal goal of graduation. They didn't know that I was a mother who had to balance a ball unlike theirs.

This would be a crossroad for me. As a child, I thought about how my actions would affect my parents; as a parent, I had to weigh how my actions would affect my child.

The challenges before me would be consequential, and I would weigh my moves and choices carefully. The issues for which we were fighting and the questions being asked were serious and life-changing.

We were asked to consider what we stood for and believed in and how much we were willing to sacrifice to make Howard a place we could be proud of. We were asked how we would answer our children if we did not take a stand and we did not make a difference. On that note, because I was already a mother, I decided that I would stand in solidarity. Yes, I had much to lose, but I also had much to gain. I knew "silence was consent when there's a duty to speak" because these were the words my mother spoke and the example she set.

Unlike most of my classmates, I was a mother. I had a future looking in my face. I had a duty. The Class of '68 graduated that June. Some students went on to graduate schools in medicine, social work, law, and other fields of endeavor. They would continue to make an imprint and have an input to the future classes.

The summer of '68 was my usual Howard experience. It was my last summer school. I had put it off and prayed that somehow, I would be spared my one dreaded class, swimming. Howard, like many Black colleges, knew most Black children did not have access to public pools, and so it was their mission to make certain we would have that skill. Much to my chagrin, my moment of truth was at my door.

For all the reasons many Black girls did not relish the class, I thought about my hair. How would I manage this task and keep my look? How would I survive this? Our swimming teacher was young, energetic, and focused. She instructed from our first session what the goals of the class would be and what she expected from us.

I never practiced any skill as diligently as I did swimming. Not only did I go to class, I went back to practice what I had learned. Right up there with the hair thing was the fear factor. I was absolutely afraid of drowning. I knew the teacher was an experienced swimmer, and I saw the pole she used if we were in trouble. I was not comforted. For six weeks, I endured these unwanted swimming lessons, and finally, the last day came.

Our final exam was in the pool. I jumped in, swam down half the pool, turned over, and floated my way to safety. I had made it! Then she said we had to jump off the diving board; now this was too much. A classmate asked if I was going to do it.

"No way," I said.

My teacher heard me. She said, "Jefferson, you're first."

I said, "Lord, don't let me down or drown." Once again, I made it. Finally, it was to the locker room, and I said, "Never again a pool." I passed.

My teacher once again heard me and said, "Jefferson, how do you know that?"

I said, "Miss N, don't play. Just give me a D, but I gotta get out of here." I did get a decent grade, but she knew she had not trained the next Olympic gold medalist.

It was September again. I had made it through my dreaded class, and I was a senior. My three summer schools afforded me a pretty easy schedule, so to speak. My next hurdle was to pass an English exam. No one walked without passing it. Determined not to be last minute, I took the exam the first time it was offered. My strategy was if I didn't make it, then I would be able to try additional times. Unlike swimming, I had a new game plan. Well, cheers to your girl, she passed the first time. She got an 87, which was more than she needed to pass because she was not an English major.

That first semester of my senior year went smoothly. I had a senior seminar class, which had to be taken both semesters, and the rest of my schedule was pretty relaxing. My little girl could clap for her mother because she had passed two hurdles to ensure graduation. My daughter was growing fast and, as always, she was my ride-or-die buddy. We went everywhere together. To know me was to know her. We were both headed to four. She would be four years old, and I would have graduated in four years.

My second semester would prove differently. My peers from around the world and country still felt the world we were inheriting was not the world we envisioned. Unrest at Howard was percolating. Our vision of a communal goal did not materialize. The gap was greater. Instead of a bridge, there was a wall steeper than before.

The students in the sociology department were especially perturbed. Our area of study was actually responsible for looking at the function of human society. Through our classes and field work assignment, we saw firsthand the disparities. We wanted change. Our professors prepared us academically for our pursuit, but they were unprepared for our resolve. We wanted more for our community, our people, than book knowledge and a degree. We wanted to create a world where all would be rewarded for their work, where all would be able to live the American Dream, not as it was but was it was supposed to be. That crossroad between intellect and reality would push us to take a stand, would once again have students take over buildings and put Howard University on the front page of the *Washington Post* and on the agendas of Congress.

We had a plan, an agenda soon to be put into play. Those of us involved had been given our tasks. Little did we know the price and the lies that would unfold. None of us could imagine that those who instructed us would lie on us so that they would not lose face. Yes, the Class of 1969 was about to learn the price of liberty and the cost of solidarity.

Though the takeover would be short lived, the consequences promised to be lifechanging. Howard, like many other colleges throughout the nation, was tired of the takeovers and student demonstrations. We would find out firsthand how tired they were. Our professors had turned in the names of all the students they recognized to the administration. They would show us that they were not to be challenged.

We received certified letters charging us with obstruction and disruption of the normal processes of the university. This was serious. We knew everything was on the line. Graduation, if we were found guilty, was gone. My eight semesters and three summer schools would be canceled. Our diplomas and our life goals were now in the hands of the Judiciary Committee at Howard.

Those of us who had received the letters met, and we knew that lawyers were needed if we were to have a chance.

Everything for which I had worked and sacrificed and those who had invested in me hung in the balance. That little girl who would soon turn four and whose life I held in my hands would now have to wait for the outcome.

We all scrambled to get the best lawyers we could find. We needed someone who knew the law and what we were facing. Someone who didn't owe their allegiance to Howard or the system we were challenging. My parents knew lawyers. My godmother was a lawyer. The question was who would step up for us.

At last, my father found a lawyer for me. He was his frat brother. He was all in, but he had a quiet demeanor, and I wanted fire. After all, my professor had lied on me, and I was furious. I wanted him brought down, but my attorney did not come with fire and brimstone. He did, however, come prepared. That said, one of my classmates found a tough legal genius to fight her case and speak for us. She was legendary—a graduate of Howard's law school and a force to be dealt with. She came into that hearing with all the fire and facts necessary to excoriate the members of the Judiciary Committee. She asked what kind of kangaroo court this was and whether they apprised us of the fact that our testimony could be subpoenaed into federal court. By the time she finished, all charges were dropped, all records were cleared, and graduation was back on track.

Needless to say, I felt vindicated. That lying professor had failed, and I was back on track to graduate. He still held my fate in his grasp. He was my senior seminar professor. His was the class I still had to pass. Fired up and passionate in my views, I wrote my senior paper with as much fire as the attorney had presented in her argument for us. I turned in my paper and awaited my grade on it and in my class.

It was the end of May, and my daughter had turned four. Classes were over, and my ride-or-die partner and I went to Howard's campus to see my final grades in all my classes. They were posted, so there was no need to see the professor or staff. As I looked for my ID, I found my grade was a B+. As we were leaving, fate would have him walk out of his office. He would ask if I had any questions about my grade. I would tell him if he thought I deserved an A- or better but had chosen not to give it, that was between him and his God; I could live with me and my God. I further assured him that his opinion of me meant less than nothing. My baby and I were off to the races. We had made it. She would see her "Mommie" graduate. I would be the first on both sides of my family in this generation to do so. Mission accomplished.

The students were not finished making our statement. We were going to boycott graduation. The word was out. The drumbeat was heard around the campus and world. Howard's Class of 1969 would not be there. There would be an empty campus. We'd have the last word. We'd stand our ground. We knew our worth.

The administration was in disbelief. We had challenged them, they had fought back, and we had won. Former US

Senator and Governor of New York William L. Marcy said, "To the victor goes the spoils." We were determined to have our voices heard at Howard and around the world. We knew our spotlight, and we knew how to use it. Just like the Underground Railroad, the message was out. We would show them no honor, we would take no prisoners, and we would speak with quiet dignity in a silence that could not be ignored.

The President and his staff were grappling with how they could hook us in and how they could save face. They found the answer. She was packaged perfectly. She was the Honorable Congresswoman Shirley Chisholm. Just like a smoke signal, word went out, and our class decided to walk.

June 6, 1969, was the day for which I had waited since I first stepped on Howard's holy ground in September of 1965. It was the day my village awaited and for which my mother paid. It was a victory on so many stages. We had a few invitations to give, and so I selected carefully who would get mine. I decided on my mother who had made it all possible, my stepfather who had freed her economically and supported her emotionally and otherwise, my aunt who had kept my baby so I could study knowing my child was loved and cared for, and of course my princess, my precious little girl, who was the reason I went in the first place.

Graduation day was beautiful weatherwise and memorable for all the right reasons. We had fought to make Howard a Black college concerned with and committed to excellence and a bridge that would seek to bring everyone over instead of a wall that left our community behind. Everyone was excited. Our classmates from New York were on fire. They had elected the first black Congresswoman in the history of our nation. They were hooked. She would not disappoint. My mother, the wise one, would get me a copy of her speech. I still have it.

After all the pomp and ceremony, it was time for the meal, the substance, the one we had waited for. As she stood to deliver her speech, she reflected on the last few years of student demonstrations. She chronicled our concerns and grievances, and she outlined the goals we had set. We were spellbound. She knew how to hook an audience.

The anticipation of her every word was heard in our silence, our focus, our attention. And then she brought it. She said, "If I had to choose between the administration and the students, I would choose the students." She cautioned, however, that she didn't think it had to come to that yet. The response was thunderous. We had been heard, all that we sacrificed and fought for was hailed. She was the voice for which we were waiting. She was worth the fight and worthy of our attendance.

My daughter was in my stepfather's arms as we received our degrees. Her famous words were "Mommie, I didn't see you," and my response was, "I was there."

HIS JOURNEY. MY JOURNEY. OUR JOURNEY.

By Nikki Hardwick

I walked from a clinic office on a hot summer day in total disbelief. "Yes, you are pregnant" is what the nurse said to me.

I said to her, "No, not me. Re-do the test please."

She did, and the results were the same. "Wow!" I uttered.

I called my boyfriend at the time (now my husband) and told him the news I was pregnant! The first thing I stated was that I was not keeping it. We had some harsh words going back and forth with the decision I had made. At the time, I was thirty-one years old, and we had already had a beautiful thirteen-year-old daughter. Anybody who knew me was aware I did not want any more children.

By the time I got home, my emotions were all over the place. As I sat at the edge of my bed, some kind of strange feeling started to come over my entire body. It was a "tingling" feeling that was kind of hard to describe. I honestly feel it was my spirit. I immediately called my boyfriend back and told him that I was going to keep the baby. I had a pretty good pregnancy. There were no real issues, but during the actual birth, I had an emergency C-section. After that, I had a healthy baby boy!

The first three years of his life were perfectly normal. He learned his name, the alphabet, and his numbers. Potty training was a breeze. He crawled, walked, and ran with no issues. He also had a great appetite. Then I had a mother's intuition that something wasn't quite right because even though he did everything that a toddler should be doing, he wasn't very verbal. I would tell his father that something wasn't right, and his response was that boys develop a little slower than girls. All along, I knew in my heart and spirit that something was a bit off with my son. I just couldn't put my finger on it.

I decided to put him in pre-K to see if his verbal skills would develop better. He was doing fine for the first few months. Then one day when I picked him up, his teacher informed me that she had some concerns about him and that I should have him tested through the local school district. I asked, "Tested for what?"

She said, "Autism."

I looked at her with a confused look on my face. I asked, "What is autism?" I did agree to the testing, as I already knew something was a little off with my son and I wanted answers. A group of professionals sat me and my son around a table and started asking several questions. They also gave him a series of tests. The first conclusion they came up with was that he was developmentally delayed. Then they changed his diagnosis to mild autism. The confused looked appeared on my face again, then tears started to flow down my face. This was the second to third time hearing the word autism. I had no idea what this thing called autism was, and not to sound harsh, but in my honest opinion, neither did the "professionals." When I asked them to elaborate on their diagnosis of my son, the explanation was, "It's a 'disorder.' It's not your fault." Then they sent me and my son on our way.

By this time, I was even more confused. I left the clinic in total disarray and sadness. When his father and sister came home, I shared the diagnosis with them as tears started to flow again. His dad was oblivious to the information, and I realized at that time that he didn't want to accept our son's diagnosis. Next, we all diligently started doing research on this unfamiliar word, "autism," that was affecting our loved one, but we never really came up with any real answers. The internet had some information, but nothing concrete. There was all kinds of different information that it became very overwhelming.

We all continued to try to understand what was happening as we went on with our daily lives, but days were tougher on me. While my husband was at work and the children were at school, I would completely shut down, closing my blinds, getting back into bed, and crying myself into an oblivious state. At the time, I had no idea that I was falling into a depressive state. I never shared this with anyone until years later. I just couldn't understand why him? Why me? Why us? What had I done wrong? I had so many questions and not enough answers. That's where the depression came into effect.

I started drinking heavily, and I became very bitter and angry. There would be times I would look at my son and feel so sad. I would say to him, "I'm sorry" as tears would constantly flow. This was my pattern for years. As the years went by, we would try to maintain a "normal" life, still not really understanding this thing called "autism," but we always kept our focus on him, as difficult as it was. We never gave up.

When he was about five years old, he started kindergarten. We decided to put him in a mainstream class as opposed to a special education class. Even though we didn't have all the answers, we decided to do this to see if he would be able to keep up with his peers, which he did! Even though we started off rough in the beginning with his teachers and staff at his school, he had an overall great first year of school. Unfortunately, when some people hear the word "autism" or see that a child has special needs or a disability, they assume the worst. My son's kindergarten year was the first time I witnessed the ignorance some people have with these diagnoses. It made me very angry and even more bitter because people were ready to write my son off even before they got to know him and how great of a kid he was.

This is when I realized I had to snap out of this depressed state, stop having pity parties, and put on my full-body armor of God. I had some fighting to do, not physically, but mentally, spiritually, and emotionally. I started taking better care of myself, stopped drinking so much, prayed a lot (prayer works), going to church, and journaling. I just became even more focused on my son. I knew I couldn't take care of him like he needed me to in the state I was in, and he deserved me at 100 percent. I went into Mama Bear mode. I was determined to fight a good fight, and I wasn't going to lose this battle. As his school years went on, I had to go through so many trials and tribulations that I didn't have a choice but to be strong. As the days, weeks, months went on, I never would have imagined that I had to defend a child like I had to because of their special needs/disabilities.

As my son and started our journey, I decided I wouldn't put a label on him like society suggested I do. He is just KC to us. I understand he has special needs, and no, I'm not in denial, but the label had to come off my son. It's just a personal decision. No disrespect or judgement is intended to any other families. To each their own. By the time KC reached seven years old, he started becoming more verbal. This was very exciting for us as a family because this gave us hope. We realized with much love, patience, understanding, and a lot of prayer that things were about to become better, and they did! His progress is what we called "baby steps," and we were okay with that and very grateful. Any progress was great progress to us. We started to realize that not giving up on him had paid off in such a positive way, and we started to see the light at the end of the tunnel.

One day, I had an "aha" moment. How about we stop listening to the outside world that had us focusing on what he couldn't do as opposed to what he could do? Let's give him a chance to shine and to show people how "special" he really is. After all, he is God's child. By this time, I started telling him he could do anything he wanted to if he worked hard at it. I started working with him even more diligently to reassure him of the advice I gave him. It has been very difficult at times dealing with society, therapists, teachers, administrators, and even family and friends looking at your precious child as if he/she is from another planet, not really knowing much about them but passing judgement. I would tell myself that that was their problem, not ours.

It felt good when I stopped caring what "they" said or thought about my "special" son. God blessed me with him, and God doesn't make any mistakes. This I know for sure! We as a family will embrace this Gift from God whether he has special needs or not. I have no control of what the outside world does or how they think, but when my son is with us, he's just KC. No labels. Once we stopped labeling him and trying to protect him from the outside world and just let him be the "special" kid he was destined to be, he started to become more confident in himself with his peers and people in general. Checkmate!

Let your children be their true selves. Parents, I promise they will thrive beyond your expectations. Just my humble opinion. Parents, especially moms, please listen to your gut instinct when it comes to your children, especially with their development. I'm grateful I did. I know you want what's best for your child. We all do. Life is stressful enough. Stop putting so much pressure on yourself and your child/children. I say that because when my son first got diagnosed, I let so many outside opinions into our world, not realizing that it was doing more harm than good. You don't need outsiders in your family's world day in and day out. You know what's best for your child.

As years passed, I started educating myself more, not just about autism per se, but about special needs/disabilities in general. The more I educated myself, the more I could help my son. Maybe one day I can also help other children and adults become self-sufficient, happy, honorable, respectable, outgoing people who can one day thrive in this sometimes-cruel world.

My answer from God was to teach him the exact way I taught my beautiful daughter. I understood that some areas would be more difficult than others, but I refused to put any more limitations on my son. Society had been doing enough of that. So, I would always tell him he could do anything to which he put his mind that he was really smart. Remember that consistently putting positive thoughts in anybody's mind will have a positive outcome.

Had I listened to the outsiders who expected me to have low expectations of him, my son wouldn't be thriving like he is today. The naysayers only made me work harder on my son's behalf, and we proved them wrong! I also stopped relying on so many television programs, articles, and experts' opinions all the time. It was just too overwhelming. I do realize that there's a significant amount of valuable information and resources out there. My only advice is to combine whatever professional resources your child has received with your better judgement. Also, if you feel in your heart that something isn't benefiting your child's needs, you're probably right.

Please don't get influenced by the outsiders, but if it's working for your child, that's great! Keep up the good work. I can't stress this enough: you know your child better than anyone. Always do what's best for them. My son has evolved so much from when he was first diagnosed. This is the hope I want to give to parents. It is very possible for your child's situation to become better. I just started taking one day at a time after I educated myself. I became very patient and believed everything that's supposed to happen for my son will happen in divine timing.

Parents, I'm not suggesting your outcome will be like ours. It may even be better. Every child and situation is different, but as long as you keep your faith and hope and continue to pray for your child's wellbeing, anything is possible, and the outcome will most likely be a positive one. What I have learned on this journey is that when you know better, you do better, whatever your circumstances. Of course, we all want our children to have happy, healthy, "normal" lives. My son will. My faith tells me so. Just keep believing your child/children will too, and it will happen.

This journey I have been on with my son has made me a better mother, daughter, and wife. My son does not even realize he's taught me so much. We both have benefited greatly while on this journey together. I have found so much strength from within that I didn't know I had, and I thank God constantly for the change He has made in me. I hold my head up high with my son alongside me with no worries, regrets, shame, embarrassment. There's no reason for any of that. He's just too awesome of a kid with whom God has blessed me and my family. He has so much potential, and I see it every day. I'm so grateful that I took the limitations off him and just let him be.

Once I got past the initial shock of his diagnosis, stopped blaming myself, and dealt with the depression and bitterness, I realized that God does not give you more than you can bear. I also started to accept that KC's diagnosis was not a death sentence or the end of the world. Life goes on, or at least it should. For me and my family, it got better. It's up to us how we fight our battles for our children. I chose to love, do the best I could, and never give up.

Parents, try not to beat yourselves up about having a child with autism, special needs, or disabilities. I initially did, but God gave me the will and tenacity to keep fighting for my son and never give up on him. Hold your head up high. Do your best to drown out the noise of this world, and I promise you things will get better for you, your children, and your family.

Unfortunately, with the research I have done, it saddens me to know that married couples have gotten divorced because of the stress of having a child/children with special needs/disabilities. Some have put them in facilities, given them up for adoption, or given custody to other family members to raise them because it's too overwhelming for them to handle. Trust me, I understand. I just want to say that my prayers go out to all. There is no judgement here. I have nothing but empathy and compassion for you. It's not easy. Fortunately, I have been blessed enough to have KC's father and sister, family members, awesome teachers and administrators, and of course God's mercy and grace to help me during our journey.

It takes a village to raise a child, especially a child with special needs/disabilities. We stuck together as family/team and did what we had to do for KC. We had some rough bumps in the road, but we had to realize it wasn't about us. It was *all* about him. So, to my families out there, I didn't do this alone. I had a pretty good support system. But overall, it's been mainly my and KC's journey. To the parents who are on this journey alone, you might be feeling anxious, depressed, overwhelmed, or just ready to give up. My advice to you is to try to find someone to talk to. In my case, I became closer to God. This is why we've had such great results.

Remember, it's always good to try and find an outlet to relieve the stress. Unfortunately, early on in my journey, mine was alcohol. I do not advise this. Whatever you choose to do, I hope and pray that everything works out for you and your family. Once I became closer to God, started my spiritual journey, and started going to church on a consistent basis, my dark days became lighter, my depression gradually got better, and the heavy drinking became less and less. I started taking care of me more.

Getting closer to God was one of the best things I could have done for myself. The more I prayed and believed in the power of prayer, the better I was able to focus on my son. It started to make sense, and I had another "aha" moment. How could I take care of my son and his needs if I couldn't take of myself. Make sense, right? I'm always thanking God for the strength and knowledge he has instilled in me throughout this journey that I'm on with my son. It hasn't been easy, but it sure has been worth it!

Life is truly a journey, and it's up to us how we choose to handle it. For me, I've chosen to continue to educate myself on the needs for my son and do my best to implement them, but also to take care of myself and remember not to put too much pressure on myself. My son will be just fine. He always has been and always will be. I just had to put my trust to in God to really believe it. Parents, I hope some of you can relate. I'm not just talking the talk, I'm walking the walk along with God right by my and my son's side. The journey is not over for us. I believe we've barely touched the surface, but with God's presence, grace, and mercy, we've only just begun, and it makes our journey that much sweeter!

LIFE AS THE FIRST GENERATION HERE

By Frank Melendez

When I think back to the first memories of my life, I remember being in diapers in a four-cornered room feeling like a caged animal. I was angry, trying to kick the door of my crib open. I didn't like the crib because I didn't know what I was going to get for that day, and I hated being stuck in there. My father was two people. Sometimes he would come to the crib to hold me, caress my face, and love me. I felt so safe. Other times, he would slap the shit out of me in my crib because he was angry. I lived in anticipation. In the crib, I felt powerless, and I couldn't wait to get out.

I can't remember where I left my glasses, but I remember my life then, full of fear and anxiety of the aggression and violence I might receive. I loved and hated my father. The good side of my father was so nice. He created an atmosphere of love, family, structure, safety, and unity. On the flip side, he created an environment of abandonment, uncertainty, terror, tension, hostility, and violence for me and my mother. It was either so sweet or so bitter. However, it didn't start off this way.

I don't know what happened to my father in his childhood. I think some of those priests got a hold of him, if you know what I mean. My father was born and raised in Guatemala and immigrated to Miami in 1963. He was twenty-three years old. His first night in America, he slept on the steps of a Catholic Church. He worked menial jobs and met an Italian woman and married her. We don't know much about this piece of his life because we found out in our forties about this marriage.

He lived in Miami for a few years, and that marriage turned sour, so he started bouncing around America. He moved to different states. His favorite city before he moved to Los Angeles was Chicago. He liked the weather, the accents, and how fast the pace was. He came to America with legal documentation, which was unheard of in those days. He was fascinated with this country. My understanding is that he left his country to flee communism, poverty, the law, alcoholism, and people who were trying to kill him. He worked to support himself and to send money home to his family. He was big on education. Knowing the English language and math were musts. I always remember my father as a hardworking man. His first job in California was grinding bumpers in Los Angeles.

There was a bakery near his work that he liked to go to in the morning and on his breaks. My mother had recently arrived in America. She would pass by the same bakery every day before she went to work. This is where they met. She was such a beautiful woman inside and out. I asked her once, "How did you end up in America?

She said, "One morning when I went to school [in El Salvador]. There was a banner in the main entrance. It said join our English and Work Program in America. I stood their amazed dreaming of what life would be like in America." In 1986, America had recently destroyed El Salvador by testing new foreign policies on the people, and the whole country erupted into the longest cold war ever. My mom said, "I wanted to see life!" She set an appointment with a counselor, and they told her about their program. "They promised that we would learn beginner/conversational English, work, and have a place to live in America." It sounded so good. She was sold and signed up.

She was nineteen when she left her country. She was courageous. She had not been exposed to too much outside of her village. She told me, "In the beginning, your father was so elegant in his speech. He spoke English so well. He really studied and practiced English before he left his country. He spoke broken English with a 'back East' accent. He would watch movies to learn conversational English. He had favorite actors he imitated. He studied Elvis Presley, John Wayne, Humphry Bogart, Anthony Quinn, and Marlon Brando, to name a few. I wanted to speak it. We used to practice together, and we enjoyed and needed each other. I loved how I felt with him, and that is what I focused on. He would tell me his strong desires to have a family and that he wanted to do this with me. He asked her to marry him." My mom said yes, and I was born one year later.

My parents could not marry right away because my father's divorce from his wife in Miami wasn't final. My siblings and I found out in our forties that he had kids with this woman as well. We never pursued meeting them. So, that was the beginning of my mother's marriage with my father and her young son, me. She started to notice that my father had a lot of issues with which she did not know how to deal. My father was dealing with extreme alcoholism and possible schizophrenia. He had a lot of baggage with him. This sweet little angel who was my mom was his way to that family life he thought he wanted.

My mother was very religious and huge on prayer. She prayed through everything. She was caught up now in a marriage with a two-sided man and an infant son. My mom was limited in what she could do because she was illegal for the first ten years of my life. My father would use his legal status as leverage on my mother. He had papers to be here and she didn't, and he would say that she would basically be nothing without him.

We had a division of legal/illegal status in the home. We already dealt with the public for not knowing English and being brown. So, it was a trip to have this type of division in our own home. I was growing up and starting to walk and talk. However, I didn't speak to anyone but my mother. We only spoke Spanish. I didn't like English, and my dad would have days where we only spoke English to each other. I hated those days.

So, here was this little brown boy who couldn't speak English sticking out like a sore thumb. I didn't know it. I was just feeling good and independent at the time. I was bullied by White kids, especially for not knowing English. It started with just being called names, but I had no idea what they were saying. I just knew the tone wasn't right. I was really hyper as a kid, and I couldn't sit still in class. I didn't understand the Pledge of Allegiance or anything they were trying to teach us. We didn't have ESL at the time in school. So, I was a headache in class, and I couldn't speak English.

These were disabilities. There were only a handful of kids in the school who didn't know English and were all put into the disability classroom. This classroom consisted of all the kids who were drooling with braces on their heads, had uncontrollable hand movements, were in wheelchairs, or caused any disruption. We were like, "What the hell are we doing in this classroom?"

Walking to school, these White kids called me a wetback and a retard and threw rocks or whatever they found on the floor at me. I told my mother, and she talked to me about all the things they did to Jesus before he was hung on the cross. She said he taught us to turn the cheek like he did for us. I tried that. She saw that the things I was telling her were true, and she started walking me to school again. The first couple of times, the kids followed but didn't say anything. Then they crossed the line, and they start yelling the same things they had to me at my mother.

I got furious really quickly. I'm not sure how the conversation went down, but at the end I told my mother, "I got this. I'm walking to school." Now they were slapping me in the back of the head and kicking me on the way to school. I turned the cheek like my mom said. Every day, it just got worse, but I wanted to walk to school. The crowd kept getting bigger, and then it also started happening at school.

There was a particular day that changed it all. I liked tether ball, and I was playing with some other kids who didn't know English. This group of White kids came up to us and told us we had to leave. We were in kindergarten, and these kids were fifth graders. I told them that this one was ours. Everyone with whom I was playing left, and the group of White kids jumped me. I felt humiliated and left alone. I told the teachers what was happening, and it meant nothing to them. It was like it was okay to do this to me. They never got in trouble.

Well, this kept going on every day. The anticipation of receiving this daily was getting to me, and I wanted it to stop. I decided that no one was going to do anything for me and that I was going to make them afraid of me like they were afraid of The Fonz. I thought about what I could do to stop them. I imagined us all being on the playground again and me doing something different than turning the cheek. I was going to scare the hell out of them. Getting ready the night before for school, I grabbed a butter knife from the kitchen, and I carefully wrapped it up in one of my mom's dishcloths.

I hid it under my pillow, and when my mom handed me my lunch pail, I put the knife in it.

I walked to school. The kids did their routine, calling me names, hitting me, and kicking me. I turned the cheek all the way to school. I went to my disability class, and then it was time to hit the playground. I took my carefully wrapped butterknife from my lunch pail, and I tucked it in my pants. I went to their tether ball court and start playing by myself because no one would join me.

Right away, I got the "What are you doing here? This is our tether ball court." They quickly started to do their thing, calling me a retard and wetback and shoving me. I was surrounded by the biggest group of White kids yet. Someone hit me in the back of the head, and I snapped back like Spiderman with my knife. I pointed the tip at all of them and told them, "*Not today!*" I aggressively threatened them with the knife and finally tried to stab one of them. Everyone ran screaming!

At that very moment, I fell in love with the feeling of instilling fear in a person. The principal came outside and slammed me down to the floor like a felon and took my butterknife. The principal told me to sit on the bench in front of his office and not to move. The way everyone was reacting made me scared, so as soon as the principal left me there, I ran home. My mom asked me, "What are you doing home from school?"

I lied to her and told her they told us to go home early today.

Soon after, the phone started ringing. It rang three times, and I answered and immediately hung up the phone. My mom asked, "Who keeps calling?"

I told her in Spanish, "Someone keeps calling the wrong number."

The school called again. This time I answered and said, "Wrong number," and the night went on like usual.

The next morning, I got up and did the same routine. I was nervous to walk to school, but I left the house. I was walking, and all the kids were standing back from me. They were still talking about me, but now they were whispering to make sure I didn't hear them. I pumped my chest out and felt like Goliath. I thought God was on my side, like he was for Goliath. Well, I got to school, and all hell broke loose.

"Where did you go yesterday?" the principal asked. "You are dangerous to this school." Somehow my dad ended up in the principal's office. They were talking, and I sat outside on the bench, more nervous than I had ever been in my life about what was going to happen to me when my father took me home. I don't know what they told my father, but what I do know is that not only did I get kicked out of the elementary school, but I was also labeled "incorrigible" and could no longer attend any school in the school district. We would have to move out of the city my parents loved. My father was extremely upset with me, and I received the beating of my life. I feel it to this day.

So, now my parents needed to find me a school that dealt with kids who did not speak English and with the incorrigible label. They were having a hard time finding me a school. My father was losing his patience trying to negotiate with schools and teachers to work with me. He got nowhere, and he took that out on me and my mom. Now the state was putting pressure on my dad that I needed to be in school, and he was furious that I was calling attention to my mother. He was afraid someone might find out that she is illegal, and if they took her from us, it would be all my fault.

Damn. I was five years old and kicked out of the whole school system. My mom could get kicked out of the country. They were looking for a city to take me into their school, I did not speak English, I was incorrigible, and Pops was taking it out on us daily. My praying mother brought our scenario to the church for group prayer. The daughter of one of the elders attended that day. After the prayer, she told my mother that her sister was a kindergarten teacher at Greenwood Elementary School in Montebello. She said she would talk to her and see what they could do. This lady was Godsent and told my mother to get ahold of Ms. Zubia. Ms. Zubia was a woman of God, spoke fluent English and Spanish, and couldn't wait to meet me.

People thought I was a mute kid because I didn't speak. Fortunately, the principal was a good Latino who agreed to meet with my mother. After an hour of speaking with my mother, I was allowed to go to school, but with one condition. Since I listened to no one, my mother would have to attend school with me. Ms. Zubia realized right away the situation my mother was in. She was a truly good Latina teacher who loved her people and wanted to be a part of this cause with us.

I felt on top of the world. I was going to a new school, and I was the only one allowed to bring my mom. I didn't realize that I wasn't allowed in school unless she was there with me. I was doing terrible in her class. She told my mother, "Because you do not speak English and did not receive a formal education yourself, you will have a tough time helping your son. He has no interest in learning English. He doesn't see the importance of it because it is not a priority in your life."

My father worked most of the day. He would come home, snap at us, go to sleep, and do the same routine. Ms. Zubia influenced my mother to learn the material I was learning to advance herself as well. I told my mom, "If I can talk with you and the church, I'm okay with not knowing English, and I don't like it anyways."

She replied, "We can't live in this country like this."

My mother's decision was that she was going to study and learn everything I was being taught so that she could help me. We started school together. We went to school every day. Ms. Zubia was very patient and gave my mother an assistant position so that she could be in the classroom. My mother helped translate because there were more kids at this school who didn't speak English. We learned how to spell and write together. We figured out math problems together, and we even memorized the Pledge of Allegiance. I was already ahead with math due to my father's incentive program of "Do these math problems or get a beat down." I was advancing fast.

One element that was very wrong though was where we now lived. We went from a small, four-unit, quiet apartment building to a big apartment building with a lot of people and a lot going on all the time. Most of the complex was occupied at the time by gang members of CHOLOS. I used to watch these guys out my window. I noticed the way they dressed, the way they combed their hair, and the way the stood under the streetlamp at night. Man, I had never seen anything like this. I would watch them carefully spray-paint their barrios on the wall. They had all the pretty girls.

My father was fascinated with mafia lifestyle, not so much for the violence but for the code they lived by. He wanted us to live by this code. My father messed up here, but when the movie *The Godfather* came out, he couldn't wait to go see it, and he took me with him. I remember the day. We went to the old theater in Whittier off Whittier Boulevard to watch *The Godfather* on a big screen. My father took me to this movie with the hopes of me understanding his lecture on family code. I caught that, but I was attracted to everything else that happened in that movie, especially, making people fear me so that no one ever thought of bullying me again. I already had a taste of this from the playground.

I also knew at that moment what I wanted to be in life. I wanted my own family so that I could be a Godfather. I wanted to be adopted by a family like Tom was accepted by the Godfather as his son, later to become the family consiglieri. My father asked me what I thought about the movie. I told him I want to be a Godfather. I was being looked out for and raised by some of the highest-profiled gang members of our community who were transitioning into Christianity. They treated me like a son. I stayed in their homes. They taught me many things that protected me in the years to come.

From this point on, life just kept unfolding into one struggle after the next. I did some things that landed me as one of the first youths, at least from my city, to be tried as an adult. I was to bounce around from different facilities until I became old enough to catch a chain to prison. I spent most of my adolescence incarcerated with the goal of having a life sentence or being dead with honor by the age of twenty-one. I trained many youths on everything in which I was trained. I never spent a day in prison. My anger turned to pain that I released fully on the world. I lived in hate and violence. I spent many years in self-deceit, drug addiction, and violence.

As the years went on, I reconnected with my Creator and begged him to change my life. I promised that if He did, I would tell the world about it. I was invited to participate in a behavioral modification test pilot program, and if I successfully completed his program, I could be home in two years. I was all in. I went from the worst patient to running all activities of the house. I was the house coordinator, which meant I oversaw everything. I gave job functions to the crews and managed the day-to-day operations of the program.

My mother continued with her education and became a proud nurse. She died in my arms at sixty-one. My father became a drug and alcohol therapist and one of the founders of Spanish AA in Los Angeles. We have a good relationship today. We found a way to forgive and love each other. My sister never was abused and earned her Master of Social Work. She is currently a supervisor for the county. Today I am drug free, a small business owner, and a realtor. My wife and I met as teenagers in that behavioral modification program and have been married for almost twenty years. We were blessed to raise a well-adjusted young lady currently attending a university. We are blessed with each other and the mercy of God to overcome our experiences.

REFERENCES

Van Der Kolk, Bessel. 2014. *The Body Keeps the Score: Brain, Mind, and Body in the Healing of Trauma.* New York: Penguin Books.

ABOUT THE AUTHORS

ABOUT THE AUTHORS

With an irrefutable passion for advocating for small businesses and entrepreneurs, **Renee Moncito** currently serves as the director of programs for the Economic Development Corporation, where she leverages more than twenty years of experience in paving the way for excellence in communities that need the most support. With a rich background in management and leadership, Renee executes with creativity and innovation, influencing organizations across diverse industries.

With a wealth of knowledge and experience, she advocates in these sectors for economic development, social service, and justice. Her diverse background allows her to connect with business leaders at all stages, equipping them with the confidence and tools they need to soar. Moncito has lived in various cities across the United States but calls Los Angeles home. She is a prayer warrior and a God-fearing woman of faith.

To connect, email her at rmoncito@gmail.com

Chaunté Humes is a world traveler, art enthusiast, avid reader, and life-long learner committed to inspiring others to be triumphant in the face of life's most difficult challenges and traumas. Born and raised in Los Angeles, Chaunté was fascinated early in life by the power of literature thanks to her parents exposing her to the neighborhood public library and investing in her joy of reading.

She holds a degree in American Studies with a minor in African American Studies from the University of California, Berkeley and a master's degree in communication management from the University of Southern California (USC). When she isn't at her computer handling the never-ending requests of her administrative job, she's journaling, reading novels, listening to literary podcasts, perfecting her self-care routines, and planning time with her loved ones. Above all, she's God-fearing and unbreakable.

To connect, email her at chumes09@gmail.com

ABOUT THE AUTHORS

Tye Grays is a survivor with a passion for bringing people together and helping others cope and conquer life's most difficult trials. She eagerly promotes self-empowerment, encourages the blessings of having unwavering faith, and naturally imparts the wisdom she's learned along the way with anyone in need of guidance. Born and raised in Los Angeles, California, she is a mother, daughter, cousin, aunt, godmother, confidant, and loyal friend.

Grays got her start in the beauty industry as a highly sought-after licensed cosmetologist, and before the age of twenty, she became a successful entrepreneur and businesswoman. You can find her leveling up and fortifying her spiritual foundation, as she understands that to thrive and live a purpose-driven life requires that you courageously defy fear and complacency.

To connect, email her at Tyeproductions72@gmail.com

Catherine Head Kirkley was born, raised, and educated in Washington, DC. She graduated from Joel Elias Springarn in 1964 and received her bachelor of arts from Howard University in 1969 and her master of education from the University of California in 1972. She taught in the Los Angeles Unified School District from February 1970 until June 26, 2022, when she retired.

She received the following recognition: Appreciation Award - Fairfax High School; Black Student Union, 1976; Outstanding Teacher - Los Angeles Unified School District; Sex Equity Award, 1986; Outstanding Teacher - Black Caucus United Teachers, Los Angeles, 1987; Certificate of Excellence – California State Department of Education and Center for Applied Cultural Studies and Educational Achievement, 1994; and Herb Alpert Teacher of the Year – Fairfax High School, 1994.

To connect, email her at catherinehhead@yahoo.com

Nikki Hardwick was born in Chicago, Illinois in 1970. She now resides in Southern California, where she has made a life for herself. She has two beautiful children and three awesome grandsons. She has never been the school type or your typical nine-to-five career woman type. She has always done things her way, even if it wasn't acceptable to her family. She knew she was different and unique as a young girl. She started to embrace it as she became older.

Nikki has a passion for being of service and doing God's will. It has never been about the money for her. She always simply followed her heart. She is a certified life coach and is certified in vegan health, nutrition, and lifestyle. She has volunteered at schools for special needs/disabled children and adults, where she has received countless awards, certificates, letters of recommendations, and job offers. She is truly blessed!

To connect, email her at hardwickj09@gmail.com

Frank Melendez became a drug and alcohol counselor at the age of twenty. He enjoys mentoring youth to new lifestyles. While he was very successful at helping the youth, he did not have the degrees needed to get into the better income brackets in comparison to those who did have the degree. For ten years, Frank worked as an account executive for Fortune 500 companies and was always among the top-ten performers wherever he went.

Although these positions required a bachelor's degree, they made an exception to hire him. For years, he outperformed sales quotas and hit financial ceilings. He is currently a good-standing member of The California Association of Realtors and The National Board of Realtors. He would like to find a way to give back what he has learned with the hopes of youth saving time and pain in their lives. He gives all the credit to his Creator!

To connect, email him at thinkoffrank@gmail.com

publish your gift

CREATING DISTINCTIVE BOOKS
FOR LEADERS AT THE TOP OF THEIR FIELD

We're a collaborative group of creative masterminds
with a mission to empower leaders to share their unique
knowledge, insights, and experiences with the world.

Our expertise bridges the gap between
their knowledge and their readers—delivering impactful
self-help books that inspire lasting growth and change.

Want to know more?
Write to us at info@publishyourgift.com
or call (888) 949-6228

Discover great books, authors, and more at
www.PublishYourGift.com

Connect with us on social media

@publishyourgift